260 BEST INSPIRATIONAL BUSINESS QUOTES

Motivation to Get You Through Another 52 Workweeks

BY BRAD CARL

www.BradCarl.com

Greetings to you, lovers of motivation and a positive outlook!

Over the years I've become an enormous fan of inspirational quotes. There's something undeniably powerful about reading or hearing a sentence or two that makes you stop and think.

Extensive research has been done on every quotation in this book in an attempt to give proper credit where it is due. Some of the passages do not list a name along side. This is because there is no one person who can be connected to that saying.

Why 260, you ask? The number was derived from 5 workdays in a week and 52 weeks in a year. Sure we all get days off in there, some more than others. But 260 felt like a reasonable number compared to 365, the number of days in a year. I didn't want to dilute the book's quality by filling it up with quotes just to reach a number.

I feel strongly that this is a top-notch collection of inspirational quotes. (It's possible I'm biased.) The content varies

- leadership, listening, goals, sales, buying, customer service, management, success, happiness, etc. Although the title of the compilation refers to "business," the book's content applies to everyone from athletes, CEO's, managers, students - and maybe even children.

When you've finished reading this book, I'd love to hear which ones were your favorites. I am also well aware there are plenty more inspirational quotations out there. Feel free to drop me a line and let me know what you liked, what you didn't like, and what ones you like that didn't make it inside this book.

Brad Carl

Brad@bradcarl.com

P.S. - Don't forget about the BONUS at the end of the book!

P.P.S - Please use the Notes pages in the back as you see fit for your own personal use.

"Doing what you like is freedom. Liking what you do is happiness." - Frank Tyger

"The best sales pitch is no sales pitch at all."

"Never ruin an apology with an excuse."

"Opportunity is missed by most people because it is dressed in overalls and looks like work." - Thomas Edison

"Never trust someone who doesn't trust

anyone." - Brad Carl

Yes, I'm quoting myself a few times in this book. I
shamelessly apologize. You have to admit, this one has merit. It's
natural to not trust people you don't know. But you will come
across people in life (if you haven't already) that are so
untrusting, you can't help but be suspicious of *them*. What are *they*
hiding?

"You are what you repeatedly do. Excellence is not an event - it is a habit." - Aristotle

"The fish stinks from the head."

"Real knowledge is to know the extent of one's ignorance." - Confucius

I believe we often forget how imperfect we are as human beings. Being cognizant of our own shortcomings is a brilliant step in the right direction - one of tolerance.

"Most of us know how to say nothing; few of us know when."

"Do one thing every day that scares you." -

Mary Schmich

"Never let the facts get in the way of the

truth."

"Focus on where you want to go, not where you currently are."

"Life is like business; it's 20% what happens

to you and 80% how you respond."

I wish I would've learned at an earlier age that the only thing I can control is how I react to things.

"Your past was never a mistake if you

learned from it."

"Life is like photography. You need the

negatives to develop."

"Two captains sink the ship." - Turkish

Proverb

So simple yet so brilliant. What this proverb doesn't tell us is that it's okay for the lone captain to not have all the answers and to instead seek advice from those closest to him or her. This is leadership in its rawest form, folks.

"Pride comes before a fall."

"When you try to please everybody, you end

up pleasing nobody."

"A meeting is an event at which the minutes

are kept and the hours are lost."

"If people are trying to bring you down, it

only means you're above them."

"Wild ducks make a lot of noise, but they also have the sense to benefit from occasionally flying in formation."

"A consultant is someone who takes the

watch off your wrist and tells you the time."

I could go on and on about consultants, but I think this quote sums it up rather well. You already have most of the answers. Why pay someone to tell you things you know?

"I know one thing, that I know nothing." -

Socrates

"The two most common elements in the world

are hydrogen and stupidity."

"People know you for what you've done, not

for what you plan to do."

"Handle your business without people

knowing your business."

"How can there be so much difference between

a day off and an off day?"

"Look in the mirror...that's your competition."

"A smart salesperson listens to emotions, not facts."

Sales 101 does not teach this. In fact, I'm not even sure the intermediate class does, but it should. People buy things based on emotions. In fact, we do *a lot* of things based on emotion, don't we?

"A man without a smiling face must not open

a shop." - Chinese Proverb

"We are all like tea bags, put us in hot water, and you find out how strong we are."

"Do not regret growing older. It's a privilege denied to many."

"Take risks: if you win, you will be happy; if you lose, you will be wise."

"Your employees won't remember what you say but they will remember how you made them feel."

"Success isn't just about what you accomplish

in your life; it's about what you inspire others to do."

"Be silent and pass for a philosopher." -

Latin Proverb

"Some people forget to plant in the spring, idle away the summer hours and then expect to reap in the fall."

"A chain is only as strong as its weakest

link."

Yes, I know everyone has heard this no less then seven billion times. But how true is it? It's always true. *Always*. Businesses, coaching staffs, baseball lineups, war. This is an extremely valuable saying - don't ever forget it.

"Profits are an opinion, cash is a fact."

"Doing nothing is the hardest work of all."

"If you can't be criticized for it, it's probably not remarkable. Are you devoting yourself to something devoid of criticism?"

"There is a significant difference between a leader and a cheerleader."

"Where there is no vision, the people perish."

- Proverbs 29:18

I believe this is the only quote from the Bible that appears in this book. The Book of Proverbs is full of good - well - proverbs. It's worth the read on its own.

"Breakdowns can create breakthroughs.

Things fall apart so things can fall together."

"People will always notice the change in your attitude towards them but fail to notice it's their behavior that made you change."

Think about that one for a moment. Okay, now think about it some more.

"Work until you no longer have to introduce yourself."

"If you can't run with the big dogs, stay up on

the porch."

Here's another one that might seem like old news, but sometimes it's the ones we've heard over and over again that we ignore. If you can't stand the heat, stay out of the kitchen.

"A good salesman is one who can sell himself

before selling his products."

"Adversity is a fact of life. It can't be controlled. What we can control is how we react to it."

"The worst lies are the ones you tell yourself."

"Life is short, fragile and does not wait for anyone. There will never be a perfect time to pursue your dreams and goals."

"Anger is the emotion we snatch up to avoid less comfortable feelings, — confusion, fear, sadness."

"Fall 7 times, stand up 8." - Japanese

Proverb

"Sometimes the grass is greener on the other side because it's fertilized with a bunch of horse manure."

"In a negotiation, he who cares less, wins."

"There is only one way to avoid criticism: Do nothing, say nothing, and be nothing." - Aristotle

"The only job where you start at the top, is

digging a hole."

"Many of us believe that wrongs aren't wrong

if it's done by nice people like ourselves."

Wow. How strong of a statement is this one? Touché.

"Get into the habit of asking yourself if what you are doing can be handled by someone else."

This one is, of course, primarily for business owners and entrepreneurs who are in a growth period. It speaks to the importance of leaders staying focused on what leaders should be doing: leading.

"The customer's perception is your reality." -

Kate Zabriskie

"Even if you're on the right track, you'll get

run over if you just sit there." - Will Rogers

"Better to remain silent and be thought a fool than to speak and remove all doubt." - Maurice Switzer

"A piggy bank with 2 nickels in it makes way more noise than a full piggy bank." - Daymond John

"To stay ahead, you must have your next idea waiting in the wings." - Rosabeth Moss Kanter

"A scrap of paper and a stub of a pencil beats the best memory." - Michael Wardinski

"It is not the strongest of the species that survive, nor the most intelligent, but the one most responsive to change."

"To keep a customer demands as much skill as to win one." - American Proverb

"So much of what we call management consists in making it difficult for people to work." - Peter Drucker

Give Mr. Drucker a blue ribbon for this one.

"It is not your customer's job to remember you. It is your obligation and responsibility to make sure they don't have the chance to forget you." -

Patricia Fripp

"He knows the water best who has waded

through it." - Danish Proverb

"Nearly all men can stand adversity, but if you want to test a man's character, give him power."

"If you find yourself in a hole, stop digging."

"Careers are a jungle gym, not a ladder." -

Sheryl Sandberg

"When you walk into a room you look for the sucker. If you don't see one - the sucker is you."

"Most people think 'selling' is the same as 'talking.' But the most effective salespeople know that listening is the most important part of their job." - Roy Bartell

"Yesterday's home runs don't win today's games." - Babe Ruth

"Someday is not a day of the week." - Denise

Brennan-Nelson

"Wise people learn when they can. Fools learn when they must." - The Duke of Ellington

"Sales go up and down. Service stays forever."

"Don't try to be original, just try to be good."

- Paul Rand

"The more you say, the less people remember." - François Fénelon

"You do not lead by hitting people over the head — that's assault, not leadership." - Dwight D. Eisenhower

"You only have to do a very few things right in your life so long as you don't do too many things wrong." - Warren Buffet

"Criticism is dangerous, because it wounds a person's precious pride, hurts his sense of importance, and arouses resentment." - Dale Carnegie

"The successful warrior is the average man,

with laser-like focus." - Bruce Lee

"The simple act of paying positive attention to people has a great deal to do with productivity." -

Thomas J. Peters

It's crazy how simple and true this statement is. It's also mind-boggling that more people don't abide by it. If you're having trouble with the performance of an employee, a good place to begin looking for a solution might be with yourself.

"A professional is someone who can do his best work when he doesn't feel like it." - Alistair Cooke

This one can be taken in a number of different ways. Maybe Cooke is referring to not feeling like you want to give your best effort in a situation. Maybe you don't feel like the project warrants your best work. But you wind up doing it anyway because you're a pro. Or maybe he was thinking about the people who stay home from work because they have a sniffle or a headache. (Shrug.)

"A year from now you may wish you had

started today." - Karen Lamb

"The less people speak of their greatness, the more we think of it." - Francis Bacon

"Without deviation from the norm, progress is

not possible." - Frank Zappa

"The customer rarely buys what the company thinks it's selling." - Pete Drucker

This is one that is lost on many, many companies. I've read some accounts where it's believed this quote refers to understanding how your product is being used by your customer. But I think it runs much deeper than this.

A great way to find out what your customers are really "buying" from you is to *ask them*. Why do they buy from you? What really sets you apart from the competition? Too often we think it's our price and quality that people love about us. But what is it really? Maybe it's Martha in customer service that's always so jovial on the phone. Maybe it's the candy dish in the lobby. I know, I know. It sounds silly, doesn't it? But you'd be surprised...

"The difference between who you are and who you want to be is what you do."

"Business founded on friendship is friendship endangered, but friendship founded on business is friendship assured." - Colgate Hoyt

"Enjoy yourself. It's later than you think." -

Chinese Proverb

"Whenever you find yourself on the side of the majority, it is time to pause and reflect." - Mark Twain

"The trouble with the world is that the stupid are cocksure and the intelligent are full of doubt." - Bertrand Russell

"You can be the ripest, juiciest peach in the world, and there's still going to be somebody who hates peaches." - Dita Von Teese

"The penalty of success is to be bored by the people who used to snub you." - Lady Nancy Astor

"You miss 100% of the shots you don't

take." - Wayne Gretzky

This is such a classic quote - it absolutely *had* to be in

this book. Take a risk every now and then, okay?

"Never give an order that can't be obeyed." -

General Douglas McArthur

"The gem cannot be polished without friction,

nor man be perfected without trials." - Danish

Proverb

"It is better to fail in originality than to

succeed in imitation." - Herman Melville

"50% of something is better than 100% of nothing." - Chuck Barris

"Let your effort be louder than your mouth."

"Everyone has an invisible sign hanging from their neck saying, 'Make me feel important.'" - *Mary Kay Ash*

"It is better to wear out than to rust out." -

Richard Cumberland

"Business is more exciting than any game." -

Lord Beaverbrook

"Top salespeople understand they must learn to feel comfortable doing the uncomfortable." - Tim Sales

"Winning isn't everything, but wanting to win is." - Vince Lombardi

"Talk is cheap. Results are priceless." - Brad Carl

Stop telling me what you can do, what you should do, what you will do, or what you did. Make something happen instead.

"It's hard to lead a cavalry charge if you think you look funny on a horse." - Adlai Stevenson

"A goal without a plan is just a wish." -

Antoine de Saint-Exupéry

"If I had nine hours to chop down a tree, I'd spend the first six sharpening my axe." - Abraham Lincoln

"Judge a man by his questions, not by his answers." - Voltaire

"A leader is best when people barely know he exists, when his work is done, his aim fulfilled, they will say: we did it ourselves." - Lao Tzu

This is the quintessential definition of leadership.

"The art of being wise is knowing what to

overlook." - William James

"Bad is never good until worse happens." -

Danish Proverb

"The highest form of ignorance is when you reject something you don't know anything about." - Wayne Dyer

"Understanding does not necessarily mean

agreement."

"Perfection is the enemy of profitability." -

Mark Cuban

"Until someone says 'no' to you, you're not asking for enough." - Mark Goulston

"Only the wisest and stupidest of men never change. " - Confucius

"I am a great believer in luck, and I find the harder I work the more I have of it." - Coleman Cox

"There's a thin line between losing &

winning. Losing breeds winners. The main recipe to

success is through failures & hardships."

"If you're not a risk taker, you should get the

hell out of business." - Ray Kroc

"People perform best and deliver the best customer service when they like what they do."

"Pride is the mask of one's own faults." -

Jewish proverb

"The easiest way to find that missing

inventory is to place a new P.O."

"A man should never neglect his family for business." - Walt Disney

"You manage things; you lead people." -

Admiral Grace Murray Hopper

"Wise men are not always silent, but they

know when to be."

"The way you position yourself at the

beginning of a relationship has profound impact on

where you end up." - Ron Karr

"The virtue lies in the struggle, not in the prize." - Richard Monckton Milnes

"Focus on being productive instead of busy." -

Timothy Ferris

"Don't be afraid to take time to learn. It's good to work for other people. I worked for others for 20 years. They paid me to learn." - Vera Wang

"The stupid neither forgive nor forget; the naïve forgive and forget; the wise forgive but do not forget." - Thomas Szasz

"The greatest wastes are unused talents and untried ideas."

"It requires less character to discover the faults of others than it does to tolerate them." - J. Petit Senn

"Your number one customers are your people.

Look after employees first and then customers last."

- Ian Hutchinson

It might seem a little weird at first, but I truly believe in this mantra, and so should you. Happy employees breed happy customers. (Happy wife, happy life?)

"Success seems to be connected with action.

Successful people keep moving. They make mistakes,

but they don't quit." - Conrad Hilton

"After all is said and done, a lot more will be

said than done."

"I am more afraid of an army of one hundred sheep led by a lion than an army of one hundred lions led by a sheep." - Charles Maurice de Talleyrand-Périgord

"I have not failed. I've just found 10,000 ways that won't work." - Thomas Edison

"It is better to trust the eyes rather than the

ears." - German Proverb

"The harder the conflict, the more glorious the triumph." - Thomas Paine

"10% of conflicts are due to difference in opinion. 90% are due to wrong tone of voice."

"Experience is the name we give to our mistakes." - Oscar Wilde

"The difference between involvement and commitment is like ham and eggs. The chicken is involved; the pig is committed." - Martina Navratilova

"Under-promise and over-deliver."

We hear this one a lot, don't we? I recently read an article that claimed under-promising and over-delivering is "terrible advice." Well, I ask you this: is it better to over-promise and under-deliver?

"The key to winning is poise under stress." -

Paul Brown

"Show respect even to people that don't deserve it; not as a reflection of their character, but as a reflection of yours." - Dave Willis

"You should recognize that criticism is not always a put down. If you take it to heart, maybe it will guide the way you ought to be going." - Joseph H. Flom

"We never listen when we are eager to

speak."

"My job is not to be easy on people. My job is to take these great people we have and to push them and make them even better." - Steve Jobs

"Customers don't expect you to be perfect.

They do expect you to fix things when they go

wrong." - Donald Porter

"Arguing with a fool proves there are two." -

Doris M. Smith

"You must be fully prepared to lose a great deal in order to make a great deal."

"The best time to plant a tree was 20 years ago. The second best time is now." - Chinese Proverb

"If you hear a voice within you saying 'you are not a painter' then by all means paint and that voice will be silenced." - Vincent Van Gogh

"Don't raise your voice, improve your argument." - Desmond Tutu

"If you don't want your company to grow, be sure to focus on minor details and ignore the 'Big Picture.' It's the perfect formula for stagnancy." - Brad Carl

"I not only use all the brains I have, but all I can borrow." - Woodrow Wilson

"You know what charm is: a way of getting the answer yes without having asked any clear question." - Albert Camus

"If you wish to be out front, then act as if you were behind." - Lao Tzu

"Think of many things; do one." - *Portuguese*

proverb

"Out of your vulnerabilities will come your strength." - Sigmund Freud

"Spend a lot of time talking to customers face to face. You'd be amazed how many companies don't listen to their customers." - Ross Perot

"You have to learn the rules of the game.

And then you have to play better than anyone else."

- Albert Einstein

"The true entrepreneur is a doer, not a dreamer." - Nolan Bushnell

"One of the most important keys to success is having the discipline to do what you know you should do, even when you don't feel like doing it."

This one is very similar to the quote from Alistair Cooke, earlier. But there's something here about having the extra depth it takes to do the things no one else will - in order to be successful.

"If the plan doesn't work, change the plan

but never the goal."

"I'm only responsible for what I say, not for

what you understand."

This is a tough one; it's certainly arguable. But in theory,
I like it. I can't force you to understand my words. Heck, maybe
you're too stubborn to understand. On the other hand, if you
want me to "help you understand," I will. Just be sure to listen
while I do.

"Go where you are celebrated — not tolerated. If they can't see the real value of you, it's time for a new start."

"Everyone lives by selling something." -

Robert Louis Stevenson

Amen, brother!

"No matter what happens, it is within my power to turn it to my advantage." - Epictetus

"You can discover more about a person in an hour of play than in a year of conversation." - Plato

"Even a mosquito doesn't get a pat on the

back until he's well into his work."

"Change tends to be viewed as a threat to our

control."

"After the ship has sunk, everyone knows

how she might have been saved." - Italian Proverb

"What we fear doing most is usually what we most need to do." - Timothy Ferriss

"Many people might have attained wisdom

had they not assumed they already had it."

"You can't expect to meet the challenges of today with yesterday's tools and expect to be in business tomorrow."

"Think all you speak but speak not all you think. Thoughts are your own, but your words are so no more." - Henry Delaune

The world would be a different place if we all abided by this truth, wouldn't it?

"The purpose of a business is to create a customer who creates customers." - Shiv Singh

"Day by day, what you do is who you become." - Heraclitus

"Conformity is the jailer of freedom and the enemy of growth." - John F. Kennedy

"Every accomplishment starts with a decision

to try."

"Please think about your legacy, because you're writing it every day." - Gary Vaynerchuck

"Success does not consist in never making blunders, but in never making the same one a second time." - George Bernard Shaw

"It is not your customer's job to remember you. It is your obligation and responsibility to make sure they don't have the chance to forget you." -

Patricia Fripp

"Smooth seas do not make skillful sailors." -

African Proverb

"Nothing can stop the man with the right mental attitude from achieving his goal; nothing on earth can help the man with the wrong mental attitude." - Thomas Jefferson

"You haven't failed until you quit trying."

"Those who say it can not be done, should not interrupt those doing it." - Chinese Proverb

"Speak the truth, but leave immediately after." - Slovenian Proverb

"The first and best victory is to conquer self.

To be conquered by self is, of all things, the most

shameful and objectionable." - Plato

"When it becomes more difficult to suffer than

change - then you will change."

"The average is as close to the bottom as it is

to the top."

"Outstanding leaders go out of their way to boost the self-esteem of their personnel. If people believe in themselves, it's amazing what they can accomplish." - Sam Walton

"The best way to appreciate your job is to imagine yourself without one." - Oscar Wilde

"When pleasure interferes with business, give up business." - American Proverb

"Problems wouldn't be called 'hurdles' if there wasn't a way to get over them."

"Everyone is entitled to be stupid, but some

abuse the privilege."

"Seize the day and put the least possible trust

in tomorrow." - Horace

"Insanity is doing the same thing in the same way and expecting a different outcome."

"There's a difference between taking a calculated risk and simply making a bad decision." - Brad Carl

"If you haven't failed, you're not trying hard enough."

"Whenever an individual or a business decides that success has been attained, progress stops." - Thomas J. Watson Jr.

"You can't connect the dots looking forward;

you can only connect them looking backwards. So

you have to trust that the dots will somehow connect

in your future." - Steve Jobs

"In the past a leader was a boss. Today's leaders must be partners with their people...they no longer can lead solely based on positional power." -

Ken Blanchard

"If it doesn't challenge you, it won't change

you."

"A goal properly set is halfway reached." -

Abraham Lincoln

"Never interrupt your enemy when he is making a mistake." - Napoleon Bonaparte

The first time I saw this one it immediately became one of my all-time favorites.

"Vision without action is a daydream.

Action without vision is a nightmare." - Japanese

Proverb

"Shallow men believe in luck, strong men believe in cause and effect." - Ralph Waldo Emerson

"Everyone is a genius. But if you judge a fish by its ability to climb a tree, it will spend its whole life believing it is stupid."

"Obstacles are those frightful things you see when you take your eyes off your goals." - Henry Ford

"The less people know, the more they yell." -

Seth Godin

"No matter how great the talent or efforts,

some things just take time. You can't produce a

baby in one month by getting nine women pregnant."

- Warren Buffet

"Talk to someone about themselves and they'll listen for hours." - Dale Carnegie

"The most successful businessman is the man who holds onto the old just as long as it is good, and grabs the new just as soon as it is better." - Robert P. Vanderpoel

"Humility leads to strength and not to weakness. It is the highest form of self-respect to admit mistakes and to make amends for them." - John J. McCloy

"Surround yourself with the best people you can find, delegate authority, and don't interfere as long as the policy you've decided upon is being carried out." - Ronald Reagan

Of course, that's asking a lot from many business owners. It gets even more difficult when the policy you decided on is unreasonable or impossible to carry out. But in theory, this is great leadership advice from the former U.S. President.

"Quality is remembered long after the price is forgotten." - Gucci Family Slogan

"Success has many fathers, but failure is an orphan."

"Do you see difficulties in every opportunity or

opportunities in every difficulty?"

"When you're finished changing, you're finished." - Benjamin Franklin

"Say thank you to everyone you meet for everything they do for you." - Brian Tracy

This one is so true. For whatever reason, some of the most difficult words to come out of a person's mouth are "I'm sorry" and "thank you." They really do make a difference.

"The secret of man's success resides in his insight into the moods of people, and his tact in dealing with them." - J.G. Holland

"Never ask a group of people for their opinion. Half of them are going to be unhappy no matter what you decide. The sooner you accept this, the better. Think of the time I just saved you. You're welcome." - Brad Carl

"If you wish to make a man your enemy, tell him simply, 'You are wrong.' This method works every time." - Henry C. Link

"If you treat staff as your equal, they'll roll their sleeves up to get the job done." - John Ilhan

"A mistake repeated more than once is a

decision." - Paulo Coelho

My wife and I think this is a good one for children as well as adults. Funny how that works, isn't it?

"People sometimes attribute my success to my genius; all the genius I know anything about is hard work." - Alexander Hamilton

"The man who removes a mountain begins by carrying away small stones." - Chinese Proverb

"A budget tells us what we can't afford, but it doesn't keep us from buying it." - William Feather

"The first responsibility of a leader is to define reality. The last is to say thank you. In between, the leader is a servant." - Max DePree

"Deliver your words not by number but by weight." - Proverb

"It is good to rub and polish our brain

against that of others." - Michel de Montaigne

"Change is the law of life and those who look only to the past or present are certain to miss the future." - John F. Kennedy

"If you can't find the key to success, pick the lock."

"Those who take bold chances don't think failure is the opposite of success. They believe complacency is."

"Charisma is a sparkle in people that money can't buy. It's an invisible energy with visible effects."

- Marianne Williamson

"The biggest fear most people have is the fear of looking foolish in front of others." - Blair Singer

Such a good one; it's so true!

"Pearls don't lie on the seashore. If you want one, you must dive for it." - Chinese Proverb

"Have something to say, say it, stop talking."

- George Horace Lorimer

"Every chance taken is another chance to

win."

"It is good to learn what to avoid by studying the misfortunes of others." - Publius Syrius

"You must look into other people as well as at them." - Lord Chesterfield

"The ladder of success cannot be climbed with your hands in your pockets."

"If you can run the company a bit more

collaboratively you get a better result because you

have more bandwidth and checking and balancing

going on." - Larry Page

I know what you're thinking. Isn't this a no-brainer?
You'd think it would be, but sometimes we need to be reminded
of the obvious.

"In all things that you do, consider the end." -

Solon

"Do a good job and people will come to you with everything. Do a crummy job and people will go to great lengths to work around you." - Brad Carl

"A light heart lives long." - William

Shakespeare

"When dealing with people, remember you are not dealing with creatures of logic, but with creatures bristling with prejudice and motivated by pride and vanity." - Dale Carnegie

"It is the trouble that never comes that causes the loss of sleep." - Charles Austin Bates

"You can make positive deposits in your own economy every day by reading and listening to powerful, positive, life-changing content and by associating with encouraging and hope-building people." - Zig Ziglar

"You just can't beat the person who never gives up." - Babe Ruth

"Always mystify, mislead, and surprise the enemy if possible." - General Thomas "Stonewall" Jackson

"The measure of success is not whether you have a tough problem to deal with, but whether it is the same problem you had last year." - John Foster Dulles

BONUS

100 Bassackwards Inspirational Quotes

This extra section of silly quotes is a great way to unwind with some chuckles – for those of us who take life too seriously sometimes. (Ahem.)

***

"If you find yourself in a hole, keep digging. Nobody knows you messed up in China."

"Life is like hitting a baseball...you fail over 70% of the time."

"Just try it. You won't get hooked."

"Time heals all wounds. So give time some time."

"If you believe you're as young as you feel, stay away from school zones."

"If you never try, you'll never fail."

"If life's an uphill climb, just try walking backward."

"It's not how many times you get knocked down that counts...it's being smart enough to stay down."

"When all else fails, accept it."

"Rehab is for quitters."

"We have nothing to fear except earthquakes, diseases, poverty, and zombies."

"Work as a team. That way you'll always have someone to blame."

"You can't make people love you but you can make them fear you."

"Be the best you can be...but realize that's gonna be about average."

"Today is the tomorrow you worried about yesterday."

"Beauty is in the eye of the beholder, and in some cases the beholder needs Lasik."

"Why do today what you can put off until tomorrow?"

"Sometimes a hug is just someone's way of stealing your wallet."

"You are never procrastinating if you firmly decide not to do something."

"Ask not what you can do for your country; beg for what your government can give to you."

"A friend in need is a friend you can take advantage of."

"It only takes 26 muscles to smile, but it takes eight to punch someone in their smiling face."

"Be like a cat...sleep all day."

"What doesn't kill you today will try again tomorrow."

"All you need is determination...and luck, good looks, contacts, a goat sacrifice, and a billion dollars."

"You can do it this time! The previous 54 times were just practice."

"Life is 20% what happens to you and 80% what you drink to forget it."

"Don't be yourself...you're weird."

"Plan for tomorrow, live for today, and blame yesterday on the alcohol."

"If you give up on your dreams it may free up some time to actually get some stuff done."

"Just jump. Nobody cares."

"If you quit now just think of all the free time you'll have."

"The problem isn't that you're part of the 99%...it's that you're in the bottom 1% of the 99%"

"It's always darkest just before it goes completely black."

"Just say 'I understand' even if you don't. It'll save you a lot of time."

"It's not the size of the dog in the fight, it's how well Michael Vick has trained it."

"Keep your eyes on the stars; your feet on the ground. The closest star to you is the sun so stare directly at it."

"Set the bar low and try not to trip."

"Be the reason someone has to make an emergency trip to their therapist today."

"That's one small step for mankind and nothing for the female kind out there."

"There's no 'I' in 'team,' but there is in 'it's all your fault.'"

"Jesus never waited until five o'clock for wine."

"The world needs ditch diggers, too."

"You tried and you failed. The lesson here: don't try. "

"If you have enough patience eventually all of your enemies will die of natural causes."

"Where there's a will there's a way...and one family member who was left out of it. It's probably you."

"Give a man a fish; you feed him for a day. Teach a man to fish; he'll empty out your lake and leave you starving."

"There's no 'u' in team...because the team doesn't want 'u.'"

"Life is like a box of chocolates - you never know what you're gonna get...like anaphylactic shock from unlisted nuts."

"Strangers always have the best candy."

"Life is like walking on a treadmill: going nowhere at a predetermined speed."

"A stranger is a friend that I have yet to borrow money from."

"Winners always have a target. If you miss just tell people you were aiming someplace else."

"Don't worry. It gets worse."

"The 'L' in your luck has been replaced."

"You can do anything you set your mind to...if you were younger."

"Believing in yourself is the first step toward self delusion."

"There are no stupid questions, but there are a lot of inquisitive idiots."

"You're slowly dying. Your dreams are futile. You can be replaced."

"The light at the end of the tunnel has been turned off."

"Doing wrong things is good...it feels amazing when you don't know you're doing something wrong!"

"Doing nothing is hard - you never know when you're done."

"You miss 100% of the shots you don't take, and also most of the ones you do take...and some of the ones you make won't count."

"I'm not saying you're stupid. I'm saying you've got bad luck when it comes to thinking."

"It's a brand new morning and a brand new week. It's time to make a new set of bad decisions."

"If you're feeling like you could use a hand...look down. You have another one on your other arm."

"Walk like there's no such thing as cars. Drive like there's no such thing as pedestrians."

"Misery loves company...so find someone as miserable as you are and live miserably together."

"Broken bones will heal and with time, give you arthritis..."

"If at first you don't succeed...maybe you suck."

"Enjoy the simple pleasures in life...like feeling the wind blow gently through your back hair."

"You can't beat intelligence into the stupid, but hitting them In the head with a hammer is oddly satisfying."

"It's not the destination that counts, it's the amount of people you leave in the dust along the way."

"No one will ever figure out how miserable your life is if you keep posting happy/fun pics online."

"If opportunity doesn't knock, don't create a doorway. Opportunity is telling you you're worthless!"

"If you build a man a fire, he's warm for a day. If you set a man on fire, he's warm for the rest of his life."

"Pain is pain remaining in the body."

"Everything happens for a reason. Sometimes that reason is because you make bad decisions."

"The only consistent piece of all your dissatisfying relationships is you."

"If opportunity doesn't knock, fix your doorbell."

"To err is human. To give up is sensible."

"Don't ever stop second guessing the opposite of what you know to be true."

"When you believe a lack of ability can be overcome by doubling your efforts, there's no limit to what you can't achieve."

"Remember, no matter how alone or rejected you feel...your organs are worth a lot on the black market."

"You don't have to run faster than the bear, just faster than your friend."

"Humiliation starts at the end of your comfort zone."

"Don't worry about actually enjoying life, just make sure it looks like you do on social media."

"It could be that the purpose of your life is only to serve as a warning to others."

"Life might suck now, but eventually you will die and none of it will matter anymore."

"Be yourself...so everyone else knows exactly who to avoid."

"Any fatal dose is a lifetime supply."

"A penny saved is...not worth much."

"Always do the right thing if people are watching."

"What happens in Vegas usually ends up getting posted on social media."

"Lies can burn bridges faster than anything. Honesty on the other hand, obliterates them instantly."

"Fight your way to the middle, then coast."

"If you want to follow in your parents' footsteps, do everything they told you not to."

"Just keep working hard from the bottom and someday your dad will retire and you'll inherit his business."

"The early bird gets the worm. The late bird gets a couple extra hours of sleep."

"They say third time is a charm but this is your fourth."

YOUR NOTES

<u>YOUR NOTES</u>

ABOUT THE AUTHOR

Brad Carl is a former radio personality who still earns part of his living as a voiceover artist. Besides writing books and producing audio, Brad is also a successful businessman in the textile and packaging industry. A life-longer lover of music and pop culture, he wrote and released another great coffee table book in 2015 titled *50 Songs from the 70s & 80s That Still Hold Up*.

In addition, Mr. Carl has also authored a four-book fiction serial known as *Grey Areas – The Saga*. The pilot book was a recent Best Seller on Amazon thanks to its entertaining psychological drama, thrills, and twists. You can learn more about Brad including where to find the rest of his books by visiting www.bradcarl.com. Be sure to sign up for the Mail List so you can get special deals when new books are released.

Brad Carl currently resides in Kansas City, MO with his wife, Kristi, and daughter, Presley. The family also has a dog named Ali.